MARGIN

MARGINALIA

Wayne Burrows

PETERLOO POETS

First published in 2001
by Peterloo Poets
The Old Chapel, Sand Lane, Calstock, Cornwall PL18 9QX, U.K.

© 2000 by Wayne Burrows

The moral rights of the author are asserted in accordance with
the Copyright, Designs and Patent Act, 1988

All rights reserved. No part of this publication may be
reproduced, stored in a retrieval system, or transmitted,
in any form or by any means, electronic, mechanical,
photocopying, recording or otherwise without the prior
permission in writing of the publisher.

A catalogue record for this book is available
from the British Library

ISBN   1-871471-87-7

Printed in Great Britain by
Antony Rowe Ltd, Chippenham, Wilts.

ACKNOWLEDGEMENTS

Thanks are due to the editors of the following, where some of these poems, or versions of them, first appeared: *Poetry Review, Poetry Wales, Stand, Anglo-Welsh Review, New Welsh Review, Planet, Sheaf, Poetry London Newsletter, Interchange, Thumbscrew, Scintilla* (Usk Valley Vaughan Association); *The Tabla Book of New Verse 2000; Seren Poets One: The Bloodstream* (Seren, 1989); *Poetry Wales: 25 Years* (Seren, 1990); *The Gregory Poems 1991–1994* (Sinclair-Stevenson, 1994). Thanks are also due to the Society of Authors' Gregory Awards panel for an award made in 1991.

Mina Loy, *Songs for Joannes* from *The Lost Lunar Baedecker*, ed. Roger L. Conover (Carcanet, 1997). © The Estate of Mina Loy.

Jacques Lacan, *The Mirror-stage* from *Écrits: A Selection*, transl. and ed. Alan Sheridan (Routledge, 1977). © The Estate of Jacques Lacan.

for Suzie

Contents

page

9	**1. *STANZAS FOR THE HARP***
10	Llanddwyn
11	Wheatfield
12	Duet
14	Binary
15	Alzheimer's Rhetoric
17	A Token
18	Cyberscapes
19	After Lacan
23	Transference
24	A Recipe for Insanity
25	A Parable
27	Stanzas for the Harp
31	**2. *MARGINALIA***
32	SANDALS
33	MAGNETS
35	ENCOUNTER
36	PROMISE
37	SCALES
38	PLANET
39	CLOSURE
41	MARGINALIA
42	ORPHEUS
43	APOLOGIA
44	INTERLUDE
45	**3. *BIOLOGY LESSONS***
46	Biology Lessons
47	The Flayed Elm
48	Industrial Archaeology
49	The Dung-Beetle
50	After Englynion
52	The Raven
53	Transformation of the Mice

55 Enough
57 Menagerie
59 Wounded Knee
61 After Mallarmé
63 Elegy (RM)

64 **4. *THE BUBBLE***
65 The Bubble

1. STANZAS FOR THE HARP

Llanddwyn

After Pennar Davies

Let us now stand here, glance
through light as it enters the shallows
and shows the sun and water fused;
let us seize what their coupling
reveals to us, hold in mind
how its sparkling pewter-white
turns gold, copulates with slate-blue waves,
surges, laps around our feet
and foams where salt water ovulates stones
in the lime-washed forcefield
of the daylight moon. It exults
in our presence, reels at the touch
of our eyes on its skin, not living
as we are, but nonetheless
with a kind of life. It is blur
and motion, wash and heave
where the sun's tumescence attains
its height. Let us rejoice,
beloved, as water-sparks
flower in the reed-beds. Let us be flooded,
exorcised of all our doubt,
connected to gulls swooping low in the light,
to the herring-shoal. Let the play
of warmth on sunlit waves bring rabbits
tumbling from the warren-mouth.
All brims over like a wooden bowl
in sudden rain, its meaning
ours, ourselves its source, from ocean
to estuary, cloudscape, land,
nothing set apart from us,
from shamelessness, till we cease
to look, or lack joy in love.

Wheatfield

After Nesta Wyn Jones

Today, the whole and radiant sky
seems leaning, poised
on the docile calm
of a blackberry bush.
It is blue and glacial,
rocks on its heel
in the flattened grass
where I lick dark juices
from my finger-ends.
Far-off, all heat-haze
and yellow dust, a blond child
ransacks the picnic box,
her pale blue, gold-freckled eyes alight,
her stumblings precarious,
no weight on her feet.
Should I, like her
in the light of this, dance across
ears of swaying wheat
like the erratic
flickering cabbage-white,
leave undisturbed the brown-furred
mice at their roots,
all the stalks unbent,
till I reach her, only to find
her safe? Or, being closer,
should I leave her be,
stay content to stretch my limbs
in the autumn heat,
watch the day's wheat-stalk
wilt in my palm
then keep it, to show her,
on her return?

Duet

1.
It is noon, and lowering. Late August,
quiet. We walk among dogrose and ivy
where the open pages of a granite book
show erosion, the glutinous texts of snails,
white birdlime spattered on blackened
stone. *Here Lies... ; Sarah, Wife Of --------;*
Christ In... ; ...Sleeping... ; -----------,
Aged Nine.   You are leaning across
a tilted grave, one palm on a syllable
of someone's name. With a coffee-pot clutched
between elbow and breast
you gather blackberries from an angel's wing.
Between us, grass. Transparency.
Migrations of fauna; blackbirds; shade.
Above us a spire, its launch postponed
that light leaks through, a weathervane
pointing to North-North East
whatever the wind. And everywhere birdsong,
testing the echo of a hollow nave,
its roof laid open to the sight of God
like a gutted fish.   You dress in white,
dissolve with the world in the heat off stone
like falling water, frosted glass.
Walk towards me, pointing like a Raphael *Christ*
at the *SOL* embossed in your open palm.

2.
Red Sandstone. Marble. Brincliffe Blue.
Granite, weathered to rocksalt. Iron.
Time passes through monuments two hundred
years old, embraces millennia
of constituent rock. *Quartz and Mica,*
Feldspar, Slate. Silicates, Larkivite.
Limestone. Lead...
                Where you walk, now,
singing the moment's song, your lips
incarnadine with blackberry-juice, the earth
is moving, too slow to see. Though
no dead rest where these headstones are
you tread so lightly – almost float.
Pigeons and magpies balloon into air
like helium rising on thermals, wings –
circling stars, their shadows wash
across your brow. Are ciphers, letters.
Listen... Words.
                Carved into fossils,
holding water and moss, they imperceptibly
re-enter stone. *Dinah, Relict... ;*
Alexander, Gentleman, of Stannington Wood.
Their names are lichen, certain. Bound.

        Shall not be Severed
        Beyond this World.

Binary

She is dreaming water, her skin turned cold
as gelatine, her body a flickering
translucency barely clear of the air
it breathes. She is all reflection
and play of light, her voice a wave-form
more felt than heard. If she crosses darkness
like a jellyfish or lens escaped
from a microscope, she'll move unseen.
When she wakes, she'll wake to rain on glass,
his face in the mirror. *A veil of breath.*

Alzheimer's Rhetoric

> *'... you can see him now
> but he's not himself... '*

... a corridor
lit like an empty page
where echoes and flickerings
turn inward, cease.
Face him. Watch him drain
from his chair
like water, heavy
with winter light. Watch
features tighten
like snares on bone,
waste into innocence,
the almost-peace
of a two-year-old.
Only bodyweight keeps him here
and he sheds it
one cell, one ounce
at a time. What survives
of him now is little more
than a scrap of song
once overheard, unwinding
where open curtains
move. He is transparent,
mouthing to McCormack, Locke,
trapped on the bridge
between a chorus and verse
that might mean something
to someone else. But listen:
will the thought occur
that whatever it is
you're hearing now
may soon enough be all you know?
Will you leave on the hour,
find halted thaw,

the rain's sub-zero temperature
congenial, nearly?
And will you even notice
that bright façade
where Santa Claus and teddy-bears
mime in tableaux
to cheap cassettes
threatening, suddenly,
all you are?

A Token

from *Songs of the City of Memphis*

Snared in willow like the neck of a goose
(my lips its beak seeking bait in your hair)
my heart, lascivious to drunkenness,
will not leave the distractions of orchards
and foliage be. Each bud turns mouth,
each apple breast, each vine to arm
and rose to sex. Your brow is willow, set to snare
the goose (whose beak seeks bait in your hair).

Cyberscapes

1.
The goose moves, deep in a green ellipse
and the rest is brilliance,
a burst of light,
a shadow transfixed where thunderclouds graze
horizons of slate. Hillsides
wrung into rivers pour
cold and swirling silts out to sea.

2.
The earthworm drags its waterlogged length
from a nucleus of algae
on a mud-crack floor.
Where once a reservoir mirrored clouds
and swimmers carved out
arcs of white,
peaches sizzle in their ochre bowl.

3.
The tongue oscillates above a milky limb,
tastes salt and bitter,
of perfume, soap...
Hair coils, tickling in the crease of a groin
till head-swirl clouds and stammers,
bursts. A drop of moisture
on a belly cools: briny, gelatinous. *DNA.*

4.
You dissolve to a residue behind the eyes,
waft backward into
through yourself
like tissue dispersed, thin air congealed
in the trembling of matches,
a lighter-flare:
A lightbulb swinging. A trapeze of wire.

After Lacan

> '... *this knot of imaginary servitude that love must always undo again, or sever.*'
> Jacques Lacan, *The Mirror-stage* (1949)

1.
A door in the river
cast adrift, creaks open
through duckweed,
reflected cloud,
through a chill, green conscience
of algae, reeds –

through deep fresh-water
and refracted light
where (eclipsed by bubbles,
outblazed by eels)
leeches cling
to a *Madonna and Child*
in a sodden bandage
four hundred years old.

He knows only surface,
a tension pinpricked
with dragonflies,
his lips and reflection both shocked numb
as he gently kisses
his own thin lips...

His features scatter,
wash clear of a ring
left hollow, and listen: *echoing.*

2.
He is naked , his body shaved, redrawn
with lipstick, *kohl*,
white perfumed dust...

As red leaves sprout from arteries
he'll sink into pillows,
his contours fixed
by an orange streetlamp,
a Venetian blind.

She is with him, on him,
seeking out every chink in his skin –
hovers, humming
the unknown words of broken songs
like a powerline.

Gravity, once distilled and salved
over stomach, ribcage,
every nerve,
flows from him,
dissolves like the dark from a street
where sandstone warms.

He will stain insomnia
into cotton sheets,
break like water
as she presses down,

becoming, already, Other. *Her.*

3.
He dreams of frail, contorted forms
(firm to the eye, like membrane to touch)

that pass for trees in lifeless woods
where chainsaws sing like skeletal birds;

moves on quickly, feels every breath
snarl and rattle in his hollow ribs

like a grain of caustic; cobalt dust
in an oyster-shell. Out here, not grass

but steel and stone enclosed
in alkaline crystals, a corrosion green

as the skin of a lime. Not mud,
but a poisonous orange sludge

where orange tyres, an orange pram
and the vermilion innards of a luxury fridge

congeal and rust against a concrete beach.
Out here is water primed for fire,

that burns like magnesium,
like a dying star, a tenuous beauty

malign and warped as this doll's head
buckling into molten fluid.

Her blue glass eyes are turned milk-white,
gaze out through the dazzling air

he draws deeply in. His throat is ulcerous,
a cave of pearls, blood a thickening

saline rush. His body opens, rides a wave
of *rubies, sapphires...* Zero Ground.

4.
He wakes, lifts his head to the glittering shape
of a wind-carved glacier,
a dying light,
a sea-lion plummeting like a stone through ice
where a white sun
dissolves in a tunnel of glass...

Then penguins, balancing eggs on their feet
in ranks immobilised
by a six-month night, no sound
but the wind and a deep, male voice
that tells him:
'... *few survive these trials, their mates return only
when the hatchings start...* '

He hears her footsteps on the wooden floor,
watches her face
in water-blue light
as she stands in her cardigan and motorbike boots,
says '*Let there be...* ',
whites him out. And smiles.

Transference

You take a seat in the yard
that shadows can't reach, your hair
a roost for all the light
the sun has spare. Dust-motes, particles
swarm and flare. Footballs
thump drily on the whitewashed walls
and lawnmower-hum, the dead-
afternoon, extravagant heat
of a time when – I can just recall –
my past excludes your kiss,
your nakedness, by only hours...
All desire, I aspire to trust,
your interest; you are thinking
of something – someone –
else. And because you are not
what I say you are
but wholly, irreducibly *just yourself*
there is only the waiting,
the pitch-and-toss, the three-
card brag and ambiguity
of the human heart as it moves from stasis
to the brink of change. Prised open,
slowly, like a sliding door
or flower-head – unpeeling, drenched
in a bar of light – it dithers,
beats, sits warm in its cage;
Pauses. Then reciprocates.

A Recipe for Insanity

Imagine the earth as it spins through space,
so fast you'd panic if you felt it move.
You don't. Your feet are rooted, here.
Move them. See landscapes shift round you.

Speak. You'll make things come, and go.
It's easy: *The grass. The firework-burst.*
Think of a colour, any colour but red.
Instantly visualise: *lipgloss. Blood.*

Read *'storms that scythe off rooftops
start with the twitch of a butterfly's wings'*.
Tape talk shows, game shows. *News At Ten.*
Rewind them. Watch them again. Again.

Know language means nothing, in itself.
Signified, sign. It's arbitrary.
What you're saying's conditioned by habit, power:
The water's dark. The cat's on fire.

Blackbirds are dinosaurs. This is true.
Evolution. There's fossil proof.
They strut the earth as if they own it still,
croak feebly, mock you. Live on worms.

Take all this too literally, personally.
Mix in the contents of one day's news.
Leave to stand in the way you live.
Think deeply, continually. Fall in love.

Then eliminate prejudice, defences, lies,
take a concept like Justice. The ABC.
Read history. Let the contrasts brew.
Take a walk, look around. And think it through.

A Parable

If I start to climb
the apple tree
and swing out
from a lichened bough
by the three
middle fingers
of a single hand,
defy gravity,
say, twenty feet
from earth
and slop bravado
like apple juice
in the sunlit leaves,
I'll be OK.
But think: *You'll fall.*
It's slippery.
Break your neck/arms/legs,
and then...
Then my fingers feel
less secure,
the whole tree
delicately poised
on its root;
my arm grows tired,
shoulder strains,
the windfalls bruise
a long way down.
Fall off then, stupid.
At your age, you...
But I know no better.
I cling where air
and branches thin
to twigs and leaf-stalks,
nets of wood.
In a cobalt sky

I might fall through
with trails of cloud
and chimney smoke,
birds and jetstreams,
kites, balloons,
I've access to vistas
almost mine
and listen, I tell you,
no way down.

Stanzas for the Harp

After Anon. hen benillion, *17th century Welsh.*

1.
The garden yours, you choose
nettle-leaves, blackthorn flowers,
stand them in water
in a crystal vase
by a wall full of shadows
and streaks of light;
spurn what you call
the vulgar rose, the lilies'
melodramatic symbolism,
the scarlets, whites and indigos
of a thousand years'
standing, still going strong.
Rather, you say, take
the under-flowers, the untended,
uprooted, bonfired hordes;
keep faith with poison,
thorn and sting,
the poise of the dangerous
unyielding strains
that – once barred from Eden –
are wholly ours.

2.
That Sunday, the bellropes tied
just out of reach
you strained on tip-toe
to touch them. Would swing,
you said, like Tarzan
through the after-echo
of the noise you'd make.
But settled for an amplified
Fred Astaire, clicking
boot-heels on a parquet floor;

found the building
unperturbed, so sat and crossed,
uncrossed bare legs.
Swore later that *Christ In Judgement*
stared, His gaze averted,
turned Heavenward
when you caught His eye –
flushed with sunlight,
yet brightened, and satisfied.

3.
Words leave residues, cracks
in the throat, root-
filaments frail as the locks of hair
we once exchanged,
the vows we once came here to make
while the ocean swirled open
its huge, damp mouth
to swallow the sun. *Just so*,
you said, placed your mouth on mine,
the sky in tumult,
on the verge of rain
yet dramatic, and deferent
to gravity. *Just so*,
you say, now you walk alone
where wild thyme snaps concrete
paving-slabs, salt wind
strips I-beams at the causeway's end
to a froth of rust
and you halt by a shrivelled
rosemary bush
to face an ocean, ironed featureless
as the sheets, undisturbed
on your hotel bed.

4.
My stumblings, *uhms,*
cross continents,
sweep in bit-streams
through time-zones, space.
Bounced off satellites
to your waiting ear
I inarticulate
what it was I'd meant:
*I thought um you might
like umm... so
how's it, like I mean,
you know...*
And you do know, somehow,
lower your voice,
pause briefly,
breathe echo, say:
yeah, missed you.

5.
She is trailing lace, white silks
so pure they tarnish flesh,
keeps dangling keys on a loop at her waist,
a cardboard child
for fertility. She holds a bouquet
of roses close
to the waterfall that conceals a face
no longer hers...
You lift her veil, see her abdomen
draw crimson light
through embroidered flowers,
hear, in the space between granite walls,
between *solemn vows*
and exchange of rings, an echo sustained
like an organ-note
on timbers creaking in a cradled roof –
the cry of a cousin
or in-law's child that will not settle
or be silenced, quite.

6.
Two loaves, a pound of fish, kerosene
and tea. You begrudge the cost,
plough through slush to reach home, dry off,
drink hot milk laced with Scotch
and slowly feel your own flesh
thaw. Where you walk, your footprints,
pressed clean into snow, submit to erasure
in aquarium-light. Like a ghost
you leave no trace of weight, disappearing,
soluble in this last conceit.
You await your chance to reply to this
with interest.

2. MARGINALIA

'Love --- the preeminent litterateur'
    Mina Loy, *Songs to Joannes* (1917)

1. SANDALS
If sandals slap on the ground as you walk
and handclaps, like fishtails on a marble slab,
drag echoes in the wake of heels
through canyons, where mirrored window-walls
bend beneath the weight of cloud:
Beware. The poppies you're holding now
will soon be red as fingernails,
flaunting mascaras under pollen lids.
The pale green-silver of their sunlit leaves
might curl like parchment, coarse as the skin
in the arch of your foot. And, yes,
you'll be *Celia, Stella, Corinne,*
translated from life into *Lyric Poem.*
Your flesh will rest lightly on its yellow bone,
sprinkled with jewellery, freckles,
sweat. Your hair's sprung copper, the silver coins
pressed to your eyelids like thimbles of light,
will catch and liquefy awnings, whirl,
burn bright as heliographs while market-stalls
unspool their ribbons and clothes
for your hands. Fingers may glitter, or fishscales run
clear in the air as piano-notes
played *glissando, fortissimo, scherzo* – stall –
then drop through the glacier of a hanging fifth,
minor, plangent as the chime of glass
against your teeth. When your red mouth opens
like a poppy's head, and language
articulates the sycamore-leaves, whole oceans
will flood your lungs, and say:

2. MAGNETS
We are blood in flux
and chemistry
wired through with nerves
and bathed in fluids;
are lights and offal,
gristle, ribs,
muscle, cartilege, cortex
and? Ourselves,
abandoned
to each other's sight,
touching, fused
then liquefied
in the act of love
as though our bodies,
cancelled out,
are all there is.
We are salt-grains in water,
drops of milk
fleshing the crimson
of a glass of wine.
We are dissolving,
are becoming,
are...

> *... with hair she binds*
> *& eyes surveys me,*
> *with necklace entangles*
> *& seal-ring brands me...*

We are lying together
in a clinging sheet,
open, drained,
equivalent.
Moth-wings battering
at dust in lamps
are pulses, laid shallow
in temples, wrists.

Your hands are perfumed
with garlic, milk;
our words, like magnets,
draw silence close.

3. ENCOUNTER

Among the heads of the roses as the sun went down,
where perspiring half-darkness sharpened light
and shadows tipped their hats as we passed,
your father cut steel with a thin, blue flame
on a copper stalk. A bell-curve of sparks
looped exact against trellis, steady as his hand,
leapt in the air like an oscilloscope-trace
as a dozen sine-waves splintered, burned,
were quenched in grass. He raised his visor – black glass,
brushed steel – leaned forward to offer
his open hand, its knuckles sunburnt, palms ingrained
with earth and oil. His teeth floresced
in his olive face, his hand might have swallowed
both of mine ... And look at us now. We are drinking fast
as the garden tilts, issues last, late heat
through a veil of chill. I've caught myself lighting
the next cigarette with this, stubbing a filter
while inhaling afresh. Glance round where you –
non-smoking, quiet – toy with hair like a scalded child,
smile and listen with your mind elsewhere,
a sandal dangling on your lifted foot
like a broken hinge. I'm convinced you're the one
I'll sleep with last, and turn, surprised,
to your father, you, your features drawn by candlelight
to awkward truce, and neutral ground.

4. PROMISE
It is not real.
You are taking off,
button by button,
hook and eye
by hook and eye,
your clothes, decorum,
sense of shame,
becoming, as I am,
all surface, lust,
not yourself
yet wholly you.
And what if my stomach
does distend
like the staves
of a barrel
with broken hoops,
if my temples thin
and teeth decay
to an idiot's inflamed
deep-crimson gums?
Will we still –
when this happens
in years to come –
unplug our catheters,
rise from chairs,
loosen flesh like raisin
soaked in bleach
and slowly, carefully
(in fear of our hearts)
see each other
as I see you now,
be not ourselves
yet wholly us, do this,
like this, and this,
and this? Promise,
love, you'll answer *yes*.

5. SCALES
You are here now, solid,
warm to the touch, draw from me
something I might call *love*
were I someone else
or so inclined. All morning
my sleep has mingled
with yours, drained exhaustion
through the crumpled
sheet, half-off the bed,
where your legs submerge
entangled with mine. You exhale
and turn, your arm
around me, your breath a low
hydraulic yawn as rich,
unfathomable, warm
as skin. Draped over
every chair are clothes
suffused with your presence
and perfume-spores.
Your weight in the mattress
is equal to mine, our balance
precarious as we shift in our sleep
like animals, restless
in a pair of scales. *Lacunae*
catch in the syntax of breath
like xylophones, birds
in the chimney. *A voice.*

6. PLANET

Less another country, you'd said,
your past seemed a planet so far off
it might take a lifetime
run backward to reach it again.
Moreover, you'd said, it had triple suns,
silicon-based, not carbon, life
and a methane atmosphere you could
barely breathe. Taking the hint,
I didn't ask. But tonight, after wine
and a TV meal, secure among clouds
of nicotine in a room we share,
you are hurtling towards it with a catch
in your voice, your forehead burning
in its stratosphere. Your words, too light
to escape its pull, stretch taut
in its gravity, thin and fade
like rays of light against the dusk.
It is named, explored, mapped out –
at rest. Less a planet, you say,
your past seems a comet that may return.
Each swing through your mind its orbit takes
lessens its substance, extends its flame.

7. CLOSURE
The clock scythes time
and buttercups,
clearing a circle
round your hands and feet.
Your backbone's
relaxed as the spine
of your book, your limbs
like its pages
turn gold in the sun.
If I came to you now
to kneel at your side,
red wine rocking
in a chipped, blue cup
as you peeled black sunglasses
from a heavy brow;
if you stretched upward
as I leaned down
and your tongue touched
on my dry tongue
like a wafer,
all warmth and symbolism,
its meaning
and metaphysics clear;
if only what once happened
might happen again
in threadbare sunlight
with curtains drawn,
your body open,
white limbs unfurled
in right proportion
to your head and trunk;
if loosened hands and fingertips
touched my body
as it rose and fell,
flushed red, made vulnerable
to push and cry
as a page to moisture

or plant to drought,
well *then*... But nothing.
We're both too tired,
preoccupied with the mind's junk-mail
and distracted talk.
Behind you, sage-leaves,
choked in dust and ivy-trails,
variegate,
warn of thunderstorms.

8. MARGINALIA

Trees unravel at the edge of the field
like estuaries, arteries,
tentacles lifting the moon to its hook,
clear of the *borealis*
headlamps make. Your footprints in snowfall
trail over the marsh,
leave shoes of black water
exposed on the dark –
their negatives fix in your shallow heels
as the Heavens move.
We sway, lightheaded with monoxide-fumes
and brandy-flasks, feel
the earth tilt like a silver tray
on a turtle's back, the sky
like a colander too big for the hills,
metallic and rattling
as the whole thing spins. There's a wind,
all teeth and cavities
we both walk through
where the traces of your bloodwarm voice
disperse on cold. We stumble
uphill with a violet sword
retrieved from a toybox,
knuckles whitening on each other's arms,
our footsteps brittle,
unsynchronised... Despite present tense
it's the past, of course. *Us.*
But you read, and answer: *That's not how it was.*
Maybe, once, with someone else...
Your eyelids fit like doors
in their frames. Close, chase words
to a distant source.

9. ORPHEUS

We walked to the garage to buy cigarettes,
closed and mournful, quiet as knives
in wait for flesh. '*Later*', I said,
bent to your lips as you turned aside,
'*later*', and left. But turned back once,
saw your footprints impacted in a drift of snow,
a workman shovelling coarse, blue salt.
His steel spade crunched like a tooth on stone,
levelled the traces you'd left behind.

10. APOLOGIA

Dirt creeps like sugar through veins and nerves,
heightens my body to a single itch.
I've hardly slept. The frizz
that once sanctified your auburn hair
catches up in my breathing like sawdust,
cats. Leaves me distanced, sarcastic.
Nothing's right.

> *Diascordium, mithradite, syrup of lime –*
> *for a burning fever, take an ounce of each,*
> *steep in water for a single night.*
> *In the morning, strain. Add sorrel and ale,*
> *rose-petals, marigolds, violet-leaves.*
> *Stir all together to infuse, then press...*

Your patience lost, you've 'gone to bed',
slammed the door
on conspiracies of inanimate things.
One eye, reflected in the bowl of a spoon,
stares back, accusing
through its flush of blood.
Had I the patience for utterance
or the words to try,
I'd apologise.

> *To complement, take a draught of broth*
> *strengthened with breadcrusts and chicken-stock.*
> *Add cinquefoil, borage, each single part*
> *weighed against the others in a like amount,*
> *no more together than a hand might hold.*
> *Warm through. Season. Consume at once...*

I shall come to you, humbled,
in an hour or two's time,
undress, as always, in the fumbling cold
where birdsong fills in between milkfloat and dawn.
Edge in beside you, quiet as a breath,
keeping clear of your body. My hands to myself.

11. INTERLUDE

It is dark. The city, like moonlight on water
or stars taking puddles to infinite depth
and back through time, is sparkling,
veined with the boughs of trees, squared
in the window of an unlit room
at five a.m. You are veiled in smoke
and cannot sleep, humidity weighting a sheet
round your limbs; are pacing,
unsettled, through half-light, birds,
a milk-van wheezing up a one-in-six
like an emphysemiac with a breakfast tray.
It is the anniversary of our second year
in these rooms we fill, pay dearly for,
that seem no longer enough to contain
a desire for space that thrives like bindweed
round bookshelves, clothes. You slump,
draw deep on Silk Cut, glare. Say nothing,
knowing nothing we control ourselves
can force through change. It will soon be light.
Till then, I'll hold you, my arm round
your waist, my mind on the rise and fall
of your voice as you read *The Garden of Paradise*
aloud. Moral? No moral. It ends with death.

3. BIOLOGY LESSONS

Biology Lessons

> *'... no excellent beauty that hath not some*
> *strangeness in the proportion'*
> Francis Bacon

Here is the pathos of a stuffed monkey,
a jar of eyes from a child's bad dream,
a white rat flayed on a board with chrome pins,
a thick, fruiting pungency on the air.
A child unlocks a skull, keeping count
of each bone removed, while others admire
the cells of an inner-cheek, or endure
the dissection of a freshly caught hare.

A girl wanders a line of shelves crammed
with bottles – *foetus, heart, larynx, tongue* –
her eyes careful, her hand on the clock
beating under her breast, and in her throat,
and the frail, rustling tug of her breath...
A recent hysterectomy contributes a cup
of flesh, turning slowly in a womb of glass
that bears the inverted room like a lens.

Later, in a pure silence, sunlight streams
through the still, green water of a tank
where tadpoles turn from commas to frogs.
And here is a stirring near the Wormery –
murky cortex, unwinding in a shaft of dust,
its jar a sundial, a wand of rippling light
cast between compassed initials, luminous
as an Aztec skull, a handful of fused quartz.

The Flayed Elm

The flayed elm keeps its vigil,
wades in mist. The crescent moon,
like a horned fruit hung low
in the hollow boughs, climbs slowly,
counterweight to the drowned sun
on the sky's exact scales.

A cold wind lifts its hosts –
paper, straw, leaves – takes the elm
as a mouth might a reed-pipe
(or another mouth) to breathe a tide.
A fire drifts on its raft of bark,
a bright pollen of sparks, smoke,

the crackling and kettle-whine
at the heart of the blaze, high-pitched,
almost a voice. And look!
An index-finger of flame stabbing
at stars sown in the cortex of cloud,
the moon at the top of the elm,

the dead wood crowned (stripped,
desolate), the fire at its roots
eerie in mist as a dropped halo
stammering under rain. And now this,
an earth-lunged whispering from
the close-ribbed hills: '*Come*'.

Industrial Archaeology

Imagine, ringed with fields, a crabbed city's
crumbling foundries and dark, Satanic mills,
mines and terraces worked for shadow –
leaf-skeleton, rust-flake, lichen and mould –
where in a steelworks' deserted refectory
a cat's paws fossilised in thick dust chase
a scurry of rats' feet, the scuffle preserved
where the paths cross, and continue, merged.

A frail, sickly sun bleeds through cloud,
threatening weather. *Cumulus, Nimbus* and *Cirrus*
couple on cracked slate with fungus and moss.
Exposed and rotten roof-beams ape solidity,
spotted with black rain and birds' shit,
hollow, jellied or dust from the edges in.
A tiered Iron Age fort, built to loom large
as a witness, straddles the field of vision,

dwarfs cold chimneys and dark-skinned men
gathered in backyards, allotments, fields,
fumbling with frayed straps, brass buckles
and cigarettes. Their baskets creak, coo
with cramped disquiet as wings, beaks and claws
struggle for room. When the gates give way
the birds take aim at the forged sky
and one by one the clapping clouds rise...

The Dung Beetle

After Pennar Davies

Simple, it gathers its shit in Spring
and rolls pellets of excrement to eat.
Selfless, too, sharing with feeble worms
and strong, white grubs the little it has,
fattening creatures, loaming the soil,
its tender loyalties perfected, its life
honed to a strict, prophetic round
of philanthropy and shit-shovelling.

What devotion, what humble prayers
at the altars of excrement stir
its dull, primaeval awarenesses?
Transcendence or alchemy, rolling buds
on the stalks of the early flowers,
its great work a *Genesis* of shit
that reveals, forms a fragrant rose
from the rank filth of its purpose.

A close relative, and sacred in Egypt,
Scarabaeus was the World, confidant
to the Gods as it moved through dung
with its messages, its metallic shell
and violet legs scuttling on errands
in a patient Communion with shit.
Aristophanes praised it when it freed
Peace to assume her glorious reign,

and it could fly, but preferred to keep
to its own element; rolling, tunnelling...
Its lotus-flower antennae twitch,
fumbling into light from dark manure,
and it might be deemed 'Insect of Gods'
or the 'Saintly Beetle' that reveres
and revels in the lowest of spheres,
serves the substance we most despise.

After Englynion

What's this odd, loping beast, Idwal?
it's neither insect, fowl nor fish;
a chicken's body on the feet of an eel?
or an englyn written in English?

(after Waldo Williams)

1.
A mattress of heather, sprung on ochre ground,
clings to the rock like a peal of bells;
on the harshest plateaux of sun and wind
these flowers of stone yield honey-phials.

(after Eifion Wyn)

2.
Geese break the mirrored skin of the lake,
scatter across the dawn like seed;
when nightfall stumbles on the slippery rock
they sprout, and flower in a honking cloud.

(after Euros Bowen)

3.
The ocean sweeps from the beach and spreads
the white lace hem of its silver skirt;
cold rocks tease out its glittering threads
on a curving shore, under failing light.

(after Roland John)

4.
Echoed in the mouths of the silenced dead,
constellations gleam in these overhangs;
where acres of fish slip nets of weed
oysters balance white pearls on tongues.

(after R Williams Parry)

5.
Silence travels with the dark at night
and the mountain stirs, awash with leaves;
the sun sleeps soundly on a bed of salt
while the moon lies shivering in the waves.

(after Gwallter Mechain)

6.
The night swings open on a hinge of stars,
one star remaining, like a compass-point;
at the door, the candle you hold to your face
is fixed as a nail-head, and radiant.

(after Coslett Coslett)

7.
Rain steams, thickening its muffled noise
to a thousand cramped in a milking byre;
when the slate roof's frozen, thatched with ice,
cold teats, the colour of milk, appear.

(after Ellis Jones)

The Raven

Worms, like white seed,
mine his cold flesh,
stir withered feathers,
rock the blind skull
like a hatching egg
in his body's black nest,
open the four rooms
of his congealed heart.
In his hardened veins
they whisk a black blood,
quicken the pulse
in rich, arterial seams,
spin the dark fibres
of his clenched limbs
to a white flax,
soothe the tiny brain
in all its folds, set
at peace the tight
valleys of his thought.
Emissaries of shade,
their conduct impeccable
in the vaulted nave
of his cleansed ribs,
their progress is inexorable
as the curved fern
that pushes its moist fist
against his arched spine,
its leaves like wings
still unsteady on the bone.

Transformation of the Mice

Egypt, IX Dynasty, 3686 BC
(Mus musculus conjunctiva)

Disorientated, famished,
white mice nest
in Egypt's inner-sanctum,
carry the corn-stalks
of a paltry season
through crushed ribs,
    rubble and muck,
under wires tightened
ankle-high on drawn bows,
round loose flagstones,
cave-ins, fractured skulls,
to Pharaoh or King,
a gritty, Divine meat,
the innards filed,
weighed against deed
in upturned Canopic jars,
sour, embalmed fruits
spilt on rough stone,
gnawed at tendon and vein,
    tooth and bone, all,
until the body dwells
in a scattered Heaven
of mouse-droppings. He fed
the first generation,
bred a second and third
in the thick darkness
    whose fur turned
black as caked blood
centuries old, eyes white
as albumen, jaws strong
as the cleansed bone
they ground to a white
    shadow of dust;

whose appetites focused
on inventories of gold,
the glass and stone,
the crafted Pantheon
of Crocodile and Falcon
whose true names pass
from breast to breast,
   papyrus to mouse,
pass through chromosomes
severing in a full womb;
   ... these blind mice, born
drinking a lost culture,
its relics made a cold milk
churned from carved stone.

Enough

The clatter of crockery
in a tin sink
where hairline cracks
in white tiles spread
   soft as mould
over walls immense
and stark as light,
oblivious to howling
in distant yards
where dogs proposition
and chafe at the moon...
   Enough, he thinks,
crouched by a wall,
trembling and furled
against a blue-white cold,
   more than enough,
assailed by figments
of a mind not his
that twists all shape
to *need* and *need*
when colours pour
like locusts from fire
to consume all sense
in a massive rush:
   Intense as fuck,
he'll say later,
his eyes on fire,
brain in shreds,
every snarl of perception
on the edge of collapse,
buoyed by pillows
on a bed of balloons
into mountainous cloud
as spikes, black sheets,
needles, serpents

and tarnished spoons
cling tight to his skin,
as papery faces
burnt-out by disease
loom high above him
wielding tinfoil knives...
   Enough, he thinks,
as whiteness billows
from a window
eight floors high,
thrown open on babble,
a violet sky,
late warmth, the moon
and an August breeze:

   More than enough.

Menagerie

The green iguana flicks its tongue at the glass
and locusts vibrate in their Tupperware box
as *FuturePet*'s space-age sign's belied
by threadbare carpets and peeling walls,
dayglo papers scrawled in black marker-ink
with *PYETHON OUR PRICE £80!*
    FINCH'S ONLY £5 EACH!
There's a sale on Gerbils (*including cage!*)
and Angel-Fish, parcelled into bags of six,
come *This Week Only!* with *Free Fish-Flakes!*
Pirhanas turn white scales to the light,
snap at reflections in their murky tank –
their neanderthal skulls butt a sheet of glass,
savage a chicken-leg, pierced with hooks,
sunk in water, then stripped to a bone
thin as the fingers on the clattering till
that land like flies in a pool of coins,
a beetle crunching in a spider's jaws
as she draws up scarlet knees and walks ...
There's a crinkle of cellophane, a glisten and chime
as copper bangles strike a silver watch,
as polished, maraschino nails catch light.
Outside, the rush-hour's piled up in blocks
like a child's kicked-over building bricks,
drowned out in sweat, thick steel-blue fumes
– deep bass thumps, *Eddie Grundy, Light Strings* –
in a crossfire of honking, bluster and curse
as a single, recalcitrant traffic light
keeps its eye locked open, unblinking on red.
Bells shake on mirrors in the Parrot-cage,
the Polecat strums its chromium bars...
Everywhere, squawk and whistle and growl,
wing-beat and gill-pulse, the whisper of feet;
the sweet smell of meal in a plastic bin,
the scratch of pale fingers, clang of a bell

as a girl in a fake-fur leopardskin coat
wrestles a three-tier Hamster cage
through a door-frame stuck on a *Welcome* mat.
She prises it open with elbows and feet,
slips out, blinded, as shadows cut,
sharp as black water, into concrete and light.

Wounded Knee

The plastic raft's imitation logs and twine
carry three Red Indians, wearing beads and suede,
over difficult rapids conjectured from
their kneeling postures and straining arms;
and a Chief, standing upright, ceremonially-dressed,
a tomahawk held to his musclebound chest
as he barks out orders like an Oxbridge cox.

They slide past jelly, pink salmon and crisps,
past a giant scuffed Action Man (sprawling prone
after sex with my sister's Sindy – again);
past the Tabby-Cat Mountain, curled fast asleep
at the edge of the table on a red-checked cloth.
Past salt-pots, lettuce, bundled knives and forks,
rolled pastry, tea-cups and plates of cakes,

till they come to a Chocolate Finger stockade
where the Cavalry crouches, its rifles aimed,
bogged down in a fast-setting Butterscotch cream.
The Indians halt, hold all their breaths,
make a lunge for the raised Confederate flag
when a gigantic hand, wearing one gold ring,
knocks them all into the air and shouts –

for Christ's sake can't you play somewhere else?
Next thing they know it's 'hit the floor!',
lie around scattered on its washed, red tiles,
postures frozen, paddles lost, their raft
buggered-off-with by an enormous dog
that imprints its toothmarks into every log
before proceeding to leg it, myself in pursuit.

Two weeks later the raft's found beached,
its whole crew missing, in the jaws of a Sphinx.
It chews the last corner, looks up, bored,
then skulks from the house to pester cats in the yard.
The Braves kneel forgotten by a potted plant
when their Chief is discovered with a plastic pig,
conspiring to block up the Hoover bag.

After Mallarmé

(*'Toute l'âme résumée'*)

The soul evaporates
behind the mouth,
summed up, when slowly
we breathe it out,
smoke blown through
smoke-rings – vaporised –
yet witness still
to some cigar
that consumes itself,
kissed once by fire.

Raised to the lip
between forefinger
and thumb, trembling
weightless in darkness,
a point of heat,
it brightens, fades
with each breath drawn
till, choked in ash,
it's ground to sparks
beneath the heel.

It is with me now,
pours from my nostrils
as the cancer feeds,
sings on lips, reflexive
as the wings of a fly
in a paper shade.
What pleasure there is
(slow-burning, obscure)
has eclipsed the lungs
with flowers of tar.

Exclude this. It's real
and therefore base.
Meaning, rendered
too precise, will cancel out
these precious words.

Elegy (R.M. d. 1987)

I had known you intimately, in your every cell,
every ounce of bone, had touched my hand
to your every pulse and your beating heart.
I had seen the pores of your skin adjust
and caught as you slept the growth of your hair.
I had lifted you, and felt your weight,
as everywhere within you perfect coils unfurled,
doubled on themselves, containing all life,
the blueprints of everything that ever breathed.

Now, late October, all the leaves dull gold
on a freezing wind, I take your weight again –
shoulder to wood, to the left of your head.
Move forward, slowly, over treacherous ground
to stand at the lip of a mouth in the earth.
Its warm, red clays will close on your form,
measure your shape and extent, then hollow you out
till your space remains, fixed deep in stone,
and your body-heat resurrects as coal.

4. THE BUBBLE

The Bubble

After Richard Crashaw, Bulla *(c. 1646)*

Life is short. You come of age,
shake out curves of tender flesh
and stand, defined, at the water's edge.
When Venus stepped
from the rose-pink lip
of her open shell, walked on foam
and stopped the light
for the beat of a heart,
even she, seeing you
would be speechless now.
You are dazzling, growing unseizable
as you swell to a world,
as you swoop and whirl
and hesitate, unfix the air
taking no one path.
You are veined, a glistening intoxicant,
a cloud that scatters
and rushes space,
a chaos that pursues itself
in all directions. If you pause, look down –
see the rivers flow
like blood in veins or light through blood,
slippery where sensations fuse
under wind and sun.
There's a blaze of jewels,
a deluge of flowers,
each flower a star in a grounded sky.
And now you are hovering
on the harvest-light
your body poured through an abundance
bright with all colours
as all colours merge
and torches fade. Here is the vein
of a delicate wave

stitching purple
through a wound of red;
here are the rivers, bright as milk
washing blood from the sea,
the cornfields splashing their yellow hair
in a deep blue sky.
Where wild roses open, lilies freeze,
frosting scarlet,
blushed in turn
as roses set the frost on fire
and frosts extinguish the roses' flames.
All is surface, red tinged green,
green tinted red,
all white impure
and impurity cleansed
as your bubble rises, brief as life –
a comet or a Catherine Wheel
that however the edge of its starry tail
might glide and spark
will end in an orbit all its own.